Published in 2023 by **KidHaven Publishing,**
an Imprint of **Greenhaven Publishing, LLC**
29 East 21st Street
New York, NY 10010

© 2021 Booklife Publishing
This edition is published by arrangement with
Booklife Publishing

Edited by: Emilie Dufresne
Designed by: Drue Rintoul

All rights reserved. No part of this book may be reproduced in any form without permission in writing from the publisher, except by a reviewer.

Find us on

Cataloging-in-Publication Data

Names: Gunasekara, Mignonne.
Title: Animal champions of the mountains / Mignonne Gunasekara.
Description: New York : KidHaven Publishing, 2023. | Series: Animal champions | Includes glossary and index.
Identifiers: ISBN 9781534541498 (pbk.) | ISBN 9781534541511 (library bound) | ISBN 9781534541504 (6 pack) | ISBN 9781534541528 (ebook)
Subjects: LCSH: Mountain animals--Juvenile literature. | Mountain ecology--Juvenile literature.
Classification: LCC QL113.G858 2023 | DDC 591--dc23

Printed in the United States of America

CPSIA compliance information: Batch #CSKH23: For further information contact Greenhaven Publishing LLC, New York, New York at 1-844-317-7404.

Please visit our website, www.greenhavenpublishing.com.
For a free color catalog of all our high-quality books, call toll free 1-844-317-7404 or fax 1-844-317-7405.

Photo Credits
All images are courtesy of Shutterstock.com. With thanks to Getty Images, Thinkstock Photo and iStockphoto. Throughout – totally out. Front Cover – notsuperstar, Ramon Carretero, Eric Isselee. 2–3 – soft_light. 4–5 – Lisa Stelzel, Robert Frashure. 6–7 – Daniel Prudek. 8–9 – chbaum, Chris Desborough, Eric Isselee. 10–11 – pickypalla, Pavel Svoboda Photography, Tina Andros. 12–13 – S.R. Maglione, moosehenderson. 14–15 – Ondrej Prosicky, RealityImages, Hugh Lansdown. 16–17 – Michael Roeder, Ondrej Prosicky. 18–19 – ArCaLu, Giedriius, Daria Rybakova. 20–21 – Olga Savina, Art_mriia. 22–23 – Amelia Fox, NYS, Sakura Image Inc, Monkey Business Images.

CONTENTS

Page 4 Up the Mountain
Page 5 What Makes an Animal Champion?
Page 6 Wild Yak
Page 8 Snow Leopard
Page 10 Alpaca
Page 12 Mountain Lion
Page 14 Kiang
Page 16 Eurasian Lynx
Page 18 Brown Bear
Page 20 Nubian Ibex
Page 22 Becoming a Champion
Page 24 Glossary and Index

Words that look like this can be found in the glossary on page 24.

UP THE MOUNTAIN

Living on a mountain can be difficult – it may be hard to find food, it may be cold, and it may even be hard to find a safe place to step...

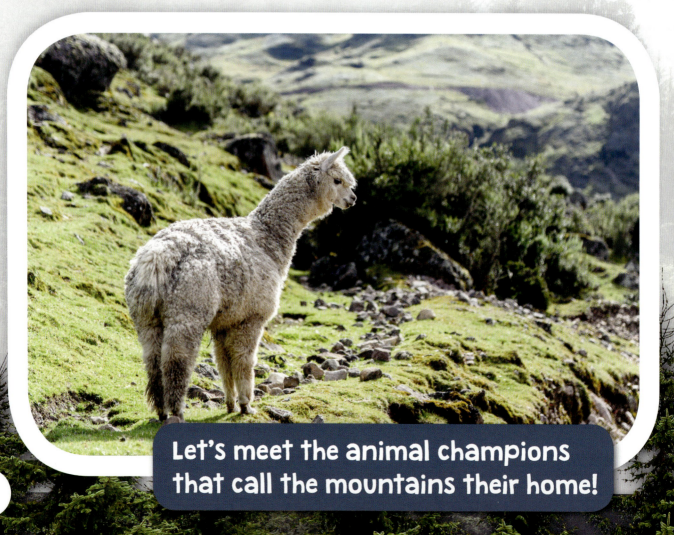

Let's meet the **animal champions** that call the mountains their home!

WHAT MAKES AN ANIMAL CHAMPION?

Animal champions don't always have to be the biggest, fastest, or strongest animals around. They are special because of the <u>adaptations</u> they have, or things they can do.

Come on! Let's head up the mountain...

WILD YAK

Wild yaks can live at heights of around 19,700 feet (6,000 m). It is very cold this high up — the temperature can dip far below freezing.

Yaks have thick fur coats that keep them warm.

Champion of Staying Warm

The air is thin at this height. This can make it hard to breathe, but yaks have an adaptation to help them. They have big lungs.

A yak's lungs can hold three times the air a cow's lungs can.

Champion of Breathing Big

SNOW LEOPARD

The colors and patterns of a snow leopard's thick fur coat allow it to blend into its rocky mountain surroundings, making it harder to spot. This is called camouflage.

Champion of Camouflage

A snow leopard's fluffy fur coat keeps it warm.

A snow leopard has a long tail that helps it balance as it climbs. It also has long, powerful back legs that help it leap really far.

Champion of Leaping

Snow leopards sometimes use their long tails as a blanket.

ALPACA

Alpacas can live at heights of up to 15,750 feet (4,800 m). Not many plants grow at these heights, so alpacas must be careful not to damage the grasses and <u>shrubs</u> they eat.

Alpacas live in <u>herds</u>.
This helps to keep them safe.

An alpaca's feet are soft and padded so they step lightly. This means they can <u>graze</u> without damaging the plants around them.

Soft foot pad

Champion of the Lightest Step

MOUNTAIN LION

Mountain lions are also known as cougars or pumas. They are fast runners and can change <u>direction</u> quickly while running because of their bendy <u>spines</u>.

Champion of Speed

Mountain lions often <u>stalk</u> animals before jumping out and killing them.

If a mountain lion cannot finish its food all at once, it will hide the food under leaves and come back to eat it later.

Champion of Hiding Food

Mountain lions are good jumpers because of their strong legs.

KIANG

Kiang can live at heights of over 13,000 feet (4,000 m), where they mostly eat grasses. When there's plenty of food, they can put on up to 100 pounds (45 kg) in body weight.

Champion of Sticking Together

There can be up to 400 kiang in one herd!

A kiang's coat changes throughout the year. In winter, it is longer, thicker, and brown in color. In summer, it is shorter, thinner, and more reddish in color.

Champion of Changing with the Seasons

EURASIAN LYNX

The Eurasian lynx lives in snowy forests. It has long legs to keep its body off the snow, and its coat grows thicker in winter to keep it extra warm.

Big, furry paws help the Eurasian lynx walk on snow.

Champion of Living in the Snow

Eurasian lynxes are very stealthy. This means they are often not seen or heard. They don't usually make sounds and they love to hide behind bushes and plants.

Champion of Sneakiness

17

BROWN BEAR

Brown bears eat a lot of food in the autumn, which makes them put on a lot of fat. The fat stored in their bodies is used to keep them going through their long winter <u>hibernation</u>.

Champion of Eating Extra

Brown bears are strong and good at digging. They dig into the mountainside to make their dens. Dens are safe spaces for them to sleep in.

They also dig into the ground to find animals to eat.

Champion of Digging

NUBIAN IBEX

The Nubian ibex is an amazing climber. It can even climb up the sides of cliffs! This helps it move around the rocky mountains it calls home while staying one step ahead of <u>predators</u>.

Champion of Climbing

The sun can be very strong up in the mountains. The Nubian ibex has a shiny coat that the sunlight bounces off of, keeping the ibex cool.

Champion of Staying Cool

BECOMING A CHAMPION

Let's see what animal adaptations we humans can use to be champions of the mountain!

A warm coat does the same job as a yak's thick fur.

Snowshoes or boots will help you walk in the snow like a lynx.

22

GLOSSARY

adaptations	changes that have happened to an animal over time that help them to be better suited to their environment
balance	the ability to stay upright
direction	the way in which someone or something is moving
graze	eat grass in a field
herds	large groups of animals that live together
hibernation	spending the winter in a very deep sleep
predators	animals that hunt other animals for food
shrubs	low-growing plants that usually have lots of stems
spines	backbones
stalk	to follow someone or something without being noticed

INDEX

breathing 7
climbing 9, 20
coats 6, 8, 15–16, 21–22
digging 19, 23
feet 11, 16
food 4, 13–14, 18
grazing 11
herds 10, 14

hiding 13, 17, 23
jumping 12–13
paws 16
running 12
sleeping 19
stalking 12
tails 9